SEYA'S SONG

BY RON HIRSCHI

ILLUSTRATED BY
CONSTANCE R. BERGUM

SASQUATCH BOOKS
Seattle

To Bernard Tom, who is gentle and kind, yet strong . . .
—R. H.

To the seyas in my life—Charlotte, Dort, Eva, Frances, Mary, and Toni.
– C. R. B.

Text copyright ©1992 by Ron Hirschi
Illustrations copyright ©1992 by Constance R. Bergum

Printed in Hong Kong
Design and title by Judythe Sieck

Library of Congress Cataloging in Publication Data
Hirschi, Ron.
Seya's song/Ron Hirschi: illustrated by Constance R. Bergum.
p. cm.
Summary: Using some traditional Clallam words, a young Indian describes the natural surroundings and activities of the Clallam, or S'Klallam, people through the seasons of the year. Includes glossary.
ISBN 0-0912365-62-5
ISBN 0-0912365-91-9 pbk
1. Clallam Indians — Social life and customs — Juvenile literature. 2. Clallam language — Glossaries, vocabularies, etc. — Juvenile literature. [1. Clallam Indians — Social life and customs. 2. Indians of North America — Northwest, Pacific — Social life and customs. 3. Clallam language — Glossaries, vocabularies, etc.]
I. Bergum, Constance Rummel, ill. II. Title.

E99.C82H57 1992   92-5029
979.7'004979 — dc20

Sasquatch Books
1931 Second Avenue
Seattle, Washington 98101
(206) 441-5555

A percentage of the proceeds from the sale of this book will benefit Port Gamble S'Klallam early-childhood programs.

ACKNOWLEDGMENTS

Many people made this book possible, especially Martha John and other S'Klallam seyas of seasons past. Myrna Milholland translated from English to S'Klallam and helped with pronunciation. Jake Jones was as invaluable to this effort as he has been in helping to preserve story and tradition for future generations.

Further assistance with manuscript review and other details related to S'Klallam people past and present was kindly furnished by Rose Purser, June Jones, Irene Purser, Shawn DeCoteau, Duane Pasco, and Jamie Valadez. Tim Secord and Don Purser offered great elk stories. Katie Sullivan's smile and her family's kindness provided much of the heart of the story. Thanks also to Edna, Skip, and Gerry.

Funding assistance was provided by Dr. Patricia Parker of the National Park Service through a Historic Preservation Grant awarded to the Port Gamble S'Klallam Tribe.

When Grandmother and Grandfather were young, S'Klallam words were with us like the wind, the songs of birds, and the swirl of the tide. Our voices were the only human sound—gentle and kind, yet strong voices that were one with the seasons of salmon and cedar.

Today, as I walk along the morning stream on my path down to the sea, I hear the sounds of S'Klallam words Grandmother (**Seya**) taught me.

Baby salmon (**kwitchin**) swim along a path all their own. They wiggle up from the stream gravel where they are born in early spring, then begin a long journey within mossy shadows of fallen logs and towering cedar (**tsshai**) trees.

The tiny silver fish swim through Beaver's (**Skio**) pond, where Heron (**Siehu**) and Otter (**Skaatl**) hunt with keen eyes. The old cedar trees shelter the baby fish just as Seya protects me and my friends.

Salmonberries (**alelo**) ripen in the sun
(**sushatsht**) as summer draws near. The purple

flowers blossom like stars (**tetosena**) along
the riverbank.

Some of the blossoms drop into the water, swirling downstream where they settle in quiet pools. The baby salmon swim downstream too, into the marshy shallows of the bay. Here is where we gather sweet-smelling grass for baskets (**mohoi**) to hold our blackberries (**qiyaiinguh**), soapberries (**xwasum**), and mussels (**tlatsam**) too.

Before they journey out to sea (**tsat-so**), the salmon leap and splash in Nuwhq'eeyt Bay. We ride our bikes or hike into the foothills, way up where the beargrass grows in the shadows of Mount Olympus (**Memptcheton**).

As the sun warms the beach (**kokhhwengu**), we hike down to swim in the bay where paddlers ride in our cedar canoes (**soiyutl**). Seya says

a young man (**swchewus**) once called the orca whales (**kloomachin**) here. They swam together far from shore and back again.

The late summer tide sweeps out. Like a great blanket, it covers, then uncovers clams (**quahok**), cockles (**stl'lam**), and crabs (**achehe**) tucked in the sand and seaweed tangles.

We dig the clams and catch the crabs, then gather for a clambake on the beach.

When South Wind (**Tsautlunsl**) blows and maple leaves turn golden in the first crisp mornings of fall, my father (**tsut**) hunts the elk (**smyets**).

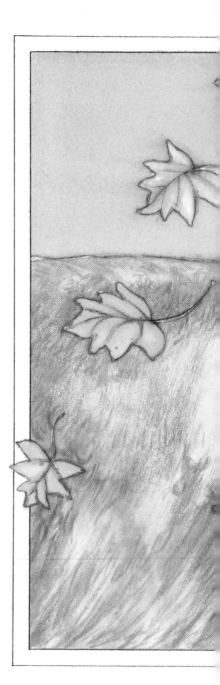

Now adult salmon (**takwaxlan**) turn back from the sea. They swim toward the streams of their birth, returning to our rivers whose names seem to sing the salmon home—Hoko, Elwha, Dungeness, Quilcene, Dosewalips, Duckabush, Skokomish . . .

Eagle (**Kwaiegsn**) waits as she has for many centuries past.

Our people wait, too. We catch the salmon in our nets.

Smoked salmon (**usxach**) will last all winter long.

We dance (**kwoieishten**), and stars come out in the nighttime sky like families gathering for our winter celebration.

I listen to the drums, watch the masked dancers, and eat the best of berry pies. My voice grows strong as I sing the S'Klallam words I learned on walks with my Seya.

Then I sleep and dream of the seasons past. Starlight and shadows dance in my mind and the words of Seya's songs—

Skio, Skaatl, and Kloomachin—swim with the tiny salmon
resting in the river, waiting for a new spring.

GLOSSARY

Try to pronounce S'Klallam words by thinking of the rain-soaked forests, tide-washed beaches, and plants and animals of the Pacific Northwest. Some of the words seem to be the very sounds produced by the song of the wind, water, or whispering wings overhead.

Chweyu, the word for whale, sounds like a gray whale spouting. Pronounce the *chw* as if reaching into your lungs to exhale as you surface after a deep dive beneath the waves. **Achehe**, S'Klallam for crab, imitates the gurgling sound made by a crab's mouth parts. Other S'Klallam words are very guttural; sounds are held and pronounced deep in the throat, especially those beginning with *q*. The hard *k* sound is there, but it begins further down than in any English word. The *ts* and *tl* sounds are made by pushing the tongue against the upper front teeth. All S'Klallam sounds are difficult for most of us. Few seyas remain who remember the words; those who do will be happy to help you. Perhaps in your search, you will help bring back forgotten S'Klallam words and songs.

Adult salmon	Takwaxlan *tuck WAH klawn*		**Clams**	Quahok *kwoke*

Adult salmon Takwaxlan *tuck WAH klawn*
This word refers to salmon on their return to the rivers where they spawn. Salmon complete their life cycle in the river of their birth and die after spawning. S'Klallam call old, dead salmon skopsh (skohpsh).

Basket Mohoi *mo HOY*

Beach Kokhhwengu *ko KWHEN go*
In the S'Klallam culture, the beach is like a city park or backyard—a center of much activity and a traditional gathering place all year long.

Beaver Skio *skee oh*

Blackberries Qiyaiinguh *kie YANG uhh*
Pronounce this word softly at the end.

Canoe Soiyutl *soy YOU tlll*

Cedar Tsshai *ts chie*
Tsshai refers to cedar wood. Siowe (see OH we) is S'Klallam for cedar bark.

Clams Quahok *kwoke*
Many kinds of clams are harvested by S'Klallam diggers, such as native littleneck, or chachnuh (cha CHA new).

Cockles Stl'lam *st LAWM*
Cockles are another variety of clam, delicious when steamed on the beach at a clambake or dried to make clam jerky.

Crabs Achehe *ah chh*
Pronounce this very softly, as if to imitate the sound of crabs bubbling and gurgling.

Dance Kwoieishten *kwoy EESH ten*
Dance and song help keep the past alive. In the Wolf (sta chng) Dance, a mask similar to that shown in the illustration of the winter celebration is worn.

Eagle Kwaiegsn *KWANGK son*
Bald eagles nest and winter throughout S'Klallam lands. They feed on salmon returning to spawning rivers.

Elk	Smyets	*smye ETS*
Father	Tsut	*tsoot*
Grandmother	Seya	*SAE yah*

This word also means grandfather and grandparent.

Heron	Siehu	*seeoh hu*

Say this word very softly, especially the ending, as if imitating the sound of wings.

Mount Olympus	Memptcheton	*MEMP t chht on*

The highest peak in the Olympic Mountains, where the mythological creature Thunderbird is said to reside.

Mussels	Tlatsam	*tl LOT smm*

Mussels grow along the upper edges of many beaches. They were probably more important in the S'Klallam diet in years past, but today they offer a valuable source of income as long as water quality can be maintained.

Nuwhq'eeyt Bay		*Na KWEET*

A small and shallow bay at the northern end of Hood Canal, also called Port Gamble Bay.

Orca whale	Kloomachin	*clue MAH chin*

Whales in general are referred to as chweyu (ch WAY ooh).

Otter	Skaatl	*ska AH tlll*

This word refers to river otters. Sea otters do not live within traditional S'Klallam lands, but river otters do, frequently swimming in the sea.

Out to sea	Tsat-so	*tsa AHHT so*

The *ts* sound is difficult but can be made by placing the tongue gently against the upper front teeth. This word means offshore, or movement away from land, not necessarily the sea itself.

River names		Hoko *(HO ko)*, Elwha *(EL wah)*, Dungeness *(DONE ge ness)*, Quilcene *(KWIL seen)*, Dosewalips *(doe see WALL ups)*, Duckabush *(DUCK a bush)*, Skokomish *(sko KO mish)*

River names in the text are current place names as used by S'Klallam and contemporary mapmakers. Many small streams also had S'Klallam names, and some of these names are being restored by tribal members.

Salmon	Kwitchin	*kweet chin*

This word refers only to spring chinook salmon, the endangered and highly prized fish that once grew to more than 100 pounds in the Elwha River.

Salmonberries	Alelo	*ah LEL loe*

Salmonberries are raspberrylike fruit the color of salmon flesh. They are fragile and usually eaten only as they are picked.

Smoked salmon	Usxach	*aah SCOTCH*
Soapberries	Xwasum	*KWAH smm*

Soapberries are small, round berries with lots of pectin. They are the main ingredient in S'Klallam ice cream, a dessert made by whipping the berries and a little sugar into a frothy mixture.

South Wind	Tsautlunsl	*t SAW tlun slll*

The winds are people to the S'Klallam and each direction is named. East Wind is Skaenet (skae NET); West Wind is Quex (k WEX); North Wind is Tsaotct (ts set).

Stars	Tetosena	*teh TOE seenah*
Sun	Sushatsht	*sue SHOT sht*
Young man	Swchewus	*shh chWAY woos*

AFTERWORD

S'Klallam people live throughout the United States, but primarily in their traditional landscape, which stretches along the shores of Hood Canal and the Strait of Juan de Fuca in Washington State. Many tribal members live on reservation lands that form a very small fraction of the total area that was once their homeland. Tribal lands and waterways once extended throughout much of northwestern Washington and parts of southwestern British Columbia.

In seasons past, S'Klallam fishermen hunted whales from sleek canoes hand-hewn from ancient cedar trees. Cedar also provided planks for homes, bark for baskets and clothing, roots for twine, and wood for paddles, boxes, and other necessities. Salmon returned to the Hoko, Elwha, and other S'Klallam rivers in great abundance during each season. Wild salmon populations included a stock of chinook salmon that grew to more than 100 pounds. Elk were plentiful. Clams and mussels grew in clean water.

Logging, dams, and pollution have all contributed to declines in fish populations. Some salmon stocks are now extinct; others are close to extinction. But S'Klallam biologists and fishermen have been leading important environmental battles in attempts to protect salmon and other valuable animals and plants for all people. Ironically, the S'Klallam and other Native Americans have been embroiled in disputes over the rights to these natural resources for many years, despite promises made to them in treaties signed by the tribes and the United States government more than 100 years ago.

Fortunately, the S'Klallam and other Washington State tribes have been working together to regain fishing and hunting rights. Historic civil rights decisions now make it possible for the S'Klallam people to harvest salmon in their usual and accustomed places. Perhaps as the S'Klallam regain rights to other resources, they will lead the way in restoring endangered species.

Maybe the S'Klallam words will help sing the animals home while seyas of all backgrounds help children remember the past, recalling for them the ways of Native American cultures—cultures dependent on healthy streams, abundant salmon, and forests filled with tall cedars and many elk. For the S'Klallam, grandparents and children are the most prized members of the community, representing as they do, the past as well as the future. Like the words in a song of life, each leads to the other and no part of the song can be left unsung. Seyas, children, salmon, cedar, and all the inhabitants of the S'Klallam world are one. Life is not possible without each of these words, each of these people, each of these animals, and each of their special places.